Cat Breeds

RAGDOLLS

BY ABBY DOTY

WWW.APEXEDITIONS.COM

Copyright © 2025 by Apex Editions, Mendota Heights, MN 55120. All rights reserved. No part of this book may be reproduced or utilized in any form or by any means without written permission from the publisher.

Apex is distributed by North Star Editions:
sales@northstareditions.com | 888-417-0195

Produced for Apex by Red Line Editorial.

Photographs ©: Shutterstock Images, cover, 1, 4–5, 6–7, 8, 9, 10–11, 12, 14–15, 16–17, 18, 19, 20, 21, 22–23, 24, 25, 26–27, 29; iStockphoto, 13

Library of Congress Control Number: 2024945505

ISBN
979-8-89250-313-6 (hardcover)
979-8-89250-351-8 (paperback)
979-8-89250-426-3 (ebook pdf)
979-8-89250-389-1 (hosted ebook)

Printed in the United States of America
Mankato, MN
012025

NOTE TO PARENTS AND EDUCATORS

Apex books are designed to build literacy skills in striving readers. Exciting, high-interest content attracts and holds readers' attention. The text is carefully leveled to allow students to achieve success quickly. Additional features, such as bolded glossary words for difficult terms, help build comprehension.

CHAPTER 1
FAMILY CAT 4

CHAPTER 2
BREED HISTORY 10

CHAPTER 3
FRIENDLY GIANTS 16

CHAPTER 4
CAT CARE 22

COMPREHENSION QUESTIONS • 28
GLOSSARY • 30
TO LEARN MORE • 31
ABOUT THE AUTHOR • 31
INDEX • 32

CHAPTER 1

FAMILY CAT

A Ragdoll cat naps on the floor. Suddenly, he hears the front door open. His family is home. The cat quickly stands up. He runs to greet his people.

Ragdolls often wait for their owners at the door.

The cat rubs his body along each person's legs. He **purrs** loudly as the family pets him. One girl picks up the Ragdoll and cuddles him.

FAST FACT

Ragdolls are usually quiet. But some make soft noises when they want attention.

Many Ragdolls enjoy being carried.

Ragdolls enjoy playing with balls, feather wands, and other toys.

Next, the girl grabs a mouse toy. She tosses it across the room. The cat runs after the toy and brings it back to the girl.

SMART CATS

Ragdoll cats are smart. They can learn how to do several tricks. For example, owners can teach the cats to play fetch or come when called.

Owners can use treats to help cats learn new tricks.

CHAPTER 2

BREED HISTORY

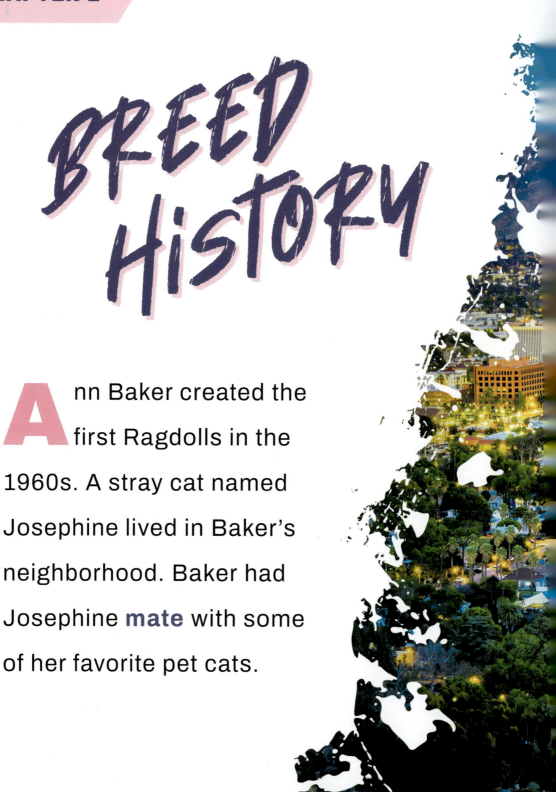

Ann Baker created the first Ragdolls in the 1960s. A stray cat named Josephine lived in Baker's neighborhood. Baker had Josephine **mate** with some of her favorite pet cats.

Ann Baker lived in Riverside, California.

Persian cats have long, soft fur. Josephine was this breed of cat.

Josephine was gentle and friendly. She had long, white fur. Many of Josephine's babies shared these traits. Over time, Baker created a new **breed**.

FLOPPY CATS

Rag dolls are toys made from cloth. They are soft and floppy. Some of Baker's cats went **limp** when picked up. So, she named the cats after the dolls.

Raggedy Ann is a famous rag doll.

Other people also began **breeding** Ragdolls. The cats spread to other countries. They became one of the most **popular** cat breeds.

FAST FACT

Because of their calm **personalities**, Ragdolls tend to be good pets for families.

The Cat Fanciers' Association made Ragdolls an official breed in 1993.

CHAPTER 3

FRIENDLY GIANTS

Ragdolls are some of the largest house cats. They can weigh up to 20 pounds (9 kg). The cats often have big, blue eyes.

Most Ragdolls are 9 to 11 inches (23 to 28 cm) tall.

All Ragdolls have long, soft fur. Many have colorpoint patterns. They have darker fur on their faces, ears, legs, and tails.

Many Ragdolls have cream-colored coats with dark-brown points.

Some Ragdolls have mitted patterns. These cats have light-colored paws.

CHANGING COLORS

Most Ragdolls have white coats when they're born. Over time, some hairs grow darker. Other parts stay light. Adult Ragdolls' coats come in several patterns.

Most Ragdolls are **affectionate**. The cats tend to have friendly and laid-back personalities. Many get along well with children or other pets.

Ragdolls are patient with small children. The cats don't mind being dressed up.

Ragdolls sometimes play in sinks, showers, or bathtubs.

FAST FACT
Many Ragdolls enjoy playing in water.

21

CHAPTER 4

CAT CARE

A Ragdoll's long fur does not shed or **mat** much. Owners should brush it once or twice a week. Some cats may need to be groomed more often.

Ragdolls tend to shed most in spring. They may need more brushing during this time.

Many Ragdolls spend a lot of time napping.

Most Ragdolls are not very active. The cats also tend to eat a lot. To help cats stay at healthy weights, owners should feed them at set times. Playtime helps cats stay healthy, too.

FAST FACT
Owners should play with their Ragdolls at least once a day.

Ragdolls may eat too much if owners leave food sitting out all day.

Ragdolls can be alone for a few hours. But they prefer to be with other pets or people. They may get lonely if left by themselves for too long.

too TRUSTING

Ragdolls tend to be very friendly. The cats may go up to strangers or wild animals. So, owners should make sure their Ragdolls do not go outside alone.

COMPREHENSION QUESTIONS

Write your answers on a separate piece of paper.

1. Write a few sentences explaining the main ideas of Chapter 3.

2. Would you like to own a Ragdoll? Why or why not?

3. When did Ann Baker create the first Ragdolls?
    - A. the 1960s
    - B. the 1980s
    - C. the 2020s

4. How might playing with a cat help it stay healthy?
    - A. Playing helps a cat stay active and not gain too much weight.
    - B. Playing helps a cat learn not to trust new people.
    - C. Playing helps a cat find lots of food to eat.

5. What does **traits** mean in this book?

Josephine was gentle and friendly. She had long, white fur. Many of Josephine's babies shared these traits.

  A. the number of babies an animal has
  B. details about how animals look and act
  C. places where animals live

6. What does **groomed** mean in this book?

A Ragdoll's long fur does not shed or mat much. Owners should brush it once or twice a week. Some cats may need to be groomed more often.

  A. brushed or cleaned
  B. covered in dirt
  C. sent outdoors

Answer key on page 32.

GLOSSARY

affectionate
Loving and friendly.

breed
A specific type of cat that has its own look and abilities.

breeding
Raising animals, often in a way that creates certain looks or abilities.

limp
Floppy or loose.

mat
To form thick, tangled clumps.

mate
To form a pair and come together to have babies.

personalities
The ways that people or animals usually act.

popular
Liked by or known to many people.

purrs
Makes a low, vibrating sound.

BOOKS

Clausen-Grace, Nicki. *Ragdolls*. Mankato, MN: Black Rabbit Books, 2020.

Jaycox, Jaclyn. *Read All About Cats*. North Mankato, MN: Capstone Publishing, 2021.

Pearson, Marie. *Cat Behavior*. Minneapolis: Abdo Publishing, 2024.

ONLINE RESOURCES

Visit **www.apexeditions.com** to find links and resources related to this title.

ABOUT THE AUTHOR

Abby Doty is a writer, editor, and booklover from Minnesota.

INDEX

A
attention, 6

B
Baker, Ann, 10, 12–13
breeds, 12, 14

C
calm, 14

F
families, 4, 6, 14
fur, 12, 18, 22

G
grooming, 22

J
Josephine, 10, 12

M
mating, 10

O
owners, 9, 22, 24–26

P
patterns, 18–19
play, 9, 21, 25

Q
quiet, 6

R
rag dolls (toy), 13

T
tricks, 9

ANSWER KEY:
1. Answers will vary; 2. Answers will vary; 3. A; 4. A; 5. B; 6. A